MW01595984

A Pocket Guide: Cultural Plants of the Lower Sioux Indian
Community

This is a second edition printing, August, 2018

ISBN 13: 978-1535545211

ISBN 10: 1535545216

Acknowledgements

This publication was made possible in part by the people of Minnesota through a grant funded by an appropriation to the Minnesota Historical Society from the Minnesota Arts & Cultural Heritage Fund. Any views, findings, opinions, conclusions or recommendations expressed in this publication are those of the authors and do not necessarily represent those of the State of Minnesota, the Minnesota Historical Society, or the Minnesota Historic Resources Advisory Committee.

A Pocket Guide

Cultural Plants
of the
Lower Sioux Indian Community

Table of Contents

Table of Contents

Table of Contents

Table of Contents

"...plants were harvested and used in such a way to ensure the physical and spiritual well-being through the Tipi Hanska Wakan, or Medicine Lodge. In earlier times of the Mdewakanton Dakota, the Unktehi Medicine Lodge was a way of life. The old people would talk of a time when medicine gathering was done by a large host of people from various bands of the Mdewakanton Dakota...They would say say that the singing of these medicine songs could be heard by people far away, and that the singing would touch the sky...The singing was honoring the lightning that returns the magic back to the earth, so that the people will live once again through the proper use of the medicine plants that were put here by the Wkan Unktehi from the beginning of time. To many of the true believers of lodge practices in earlier times, the sincerity of humbleness holds the key to the magic of the plants that are put here for the Dakota people to use in a positive way."

-Mdewakanton Sioux tribal member

Introduction

This booklet on cultural and medicinal plants of the Dakota was created to provide users with information on Native American heritage and the traditional uses of ecological resources. There is perhaps no better way to preserve a language and historical ecology than through the names and plants that were interwoven among the lives of the tribes. Plants were embedded within Native American folklore and were their pharmacy, grocery, toys, tools, fabric, dwellings, and spiritual icons. Knowledge of traditional plant use has been passed from generation to generation, and has been summarized within this booklet to serve as a guide for learners of all ages.

Background of the Greater Dakota Nation

The Lower Sioux Indian Community is a Mdewakanton band of the Dakota Sioux. It is located in Minnesota; the place where the water reflects the sky, and is the place of Dakota origin. It is a member of the Greater Dakota Nation which is comprised of seven sub-tribes who make up the alliance called the Seven Council Fires. Most of the world knows the alliance as the "Sioux." The seven tribes of the Greater Dakota are divided into three divisions. They call themselves Dakota, Lakota, or Nakota; words that mean "allies" or "friends" in all three dialects. The four bands that make up the Dakota are the Mdewakanton, the Wahpeton, the Wahpekute, and the Sisseton. The bands that make up the Lakota are the Yankton and the Yanktonay. The bands that make up the Nakota are the Teton. The tribes spoke different dialects with slight difference, and were still able to understand each other. This book represents the language of the Mdwewakaon Sioux.

Dakota Language

The name "Dakota" is derived from the word "koda" of the Santees, and "kola" of the Tetons, signifying "friend." The Dakota language is a member of the Mississippi Valley sub-family of Sioux, which is just one of forty five languages that creates the Siouan Family. It is believed that each of the forty-five languages began as one larger language that divided into subgroups over time. Language has evolved into three dialects: Lakota, or Teton; Dakota, or Santee; and Nakota, or Yankton.

In all languages the names of things form a very important class of words. The Dakota vocabulary of trees and shrubs covers nearly all the varieties which grow in their country. Their names for herbs and grasses are more limited, confined chiefly to those known to possess medicinal properties and uses for food. And while they have names for the fruits that grow in their country, they have very few specific names for flower.

Importance of Cultural Plants

The people of the Mdewakanton Sioux have always been in touch with the Earth and its dynamics. Hunting and gathering practices were and continue to be a religion and a way of life. It may best be summarized by Melvin Gilmore's Use of Plants by the Indians of the Missouri River Region, as the significance of the pasque flower is described:

"Indians generally are keenly observant of all things in nature and reverent toward them. They have reverence and affection for the living creatures, the birds and beasts, the trees and shrubs and flowering plants. They have stories and songs about most of the plant and animal forms of life with which they are acquainted.

They believe that each species has its own particular song which is the expression of its life or soul. It reminds a man of his childhood, when he wandered over the prairie hill, as free from care and sorrow as the flowers and the birds. He sits down near the pasque flower on the lap of Mother Earth, takes out his pipe and fills it with tobacco. Then he reverently holds the pipe toward the earth, then toward the sky, then toward the north, the east, the south, and the west. After this act of silent invocation he smokes. While he smokes he meditates upon all the changing scenes of his lifetime, his joys and sorrows, his hopes, his accomplishments, his disappointments, and the guidance which unseen powers have given him in bringing him thus far on the way, and he is encouraged to believe that he will be guided to the end. After finishing his pipe he rises and plucks the flower and carries it home to show his grandchildren, singing as he goes, The Song of the Twin-flower, which he learned as a child, and which he now in turn teaches to his grandchildren. Tobacco was used ceremonially and the pipe might be considered as a kind of censer. The earth was poetically and mystically regarded as Mother of all living things, all plants, animals, and human beings. The Sky likewise was regarded as Father, and the Cardinal Points as the Paths of approach of the Powers which are all about us in this world. Man is not apart from nor above nature but a part of nature. All good things in nature are his friends and kindred, and he should be friendly with all. "

The "Song of the Twin-flower" given here is translated from the Dakota language by Dr. A. McG. Beede:

"I wish to encourage the children of other flower nations now appearing all over the face of the earth; So while they awaken from sleeping and come up from the heart of the earth I am standing here old and gray-headed."

The pasque flower is the very earliest bloomer in the spring, often appearing before the snow has disappeared. This fact explains the allusion in the words 'I wish to encourage the children of other flower nations.' The entire plant is hairy, and when ripe the head is white and bushy, having the appearance of a full and heavy growth of very white hair on the head of an old man. This appearance explains the allusion in 'I am standing here gray-headed' when an old Dakota first finds one of these flowers in the springtime."

Resources

The primary resources used in the development of this book were Melvin Gilmore's "Uses of Plants by the Indians of the Missouri River Region," published in 1919, Daniel Moerman's "Native American Ethnobotany," published in1998, Linda ThioleuWin Bishop's "Watoto Unyutapi," published in 2013, and John Williamson's "An English-Dakota Dictionary," published in 1992. Ryan Dixon, a language instructor with the Lower Sioux Indian Community, provided expertise for the correct spelling specific to the Lower Sioux Community.

There are many more plants with cultural uses and Dakota names than what is identified in this book. This book focuses on the most most common plants currently found, or historically native to, the Lower Sioux Reservation. Alternate Dakota names have also been mentioned in each plant's cultural use section. For example, the elm tree's Dakota word used in this book is Pe Chaŋ; alternate spelling are Pe "The Elm," Pe Chaŋ "Elm wood," Pe ikcheka "The Common Elm." Please contact the Lower Sioux Indian Community Office of the Environment for errors or alternate spellings.

Guidelines for Harvesting

Out of reverence and respect towards the plants, we ask that you please follow these simple guidelines while harvesting:

- Always harvest in a way that allows the plant to survive and regenerate.

- Follow the 1/3 rule: always leave at least 1/3 of whatever you are harvesting to allow the plant to recover. Never collect *every* item of whatever you are harvesting (flowers, berries, leaves, entire plants, etc.)

- Take only what you need to make use of the cultural or medicinal purpose—the higher the cut, the better for the plant. For example, do NOT pull Prairie Sage up by the roots while harvesting. Use a scissors to cut it at least 1 inch above the ground.

- If the plant you have harvested is going to seed, give back to the plant by shaking the seeds over the ground where you just harvested.

- Take notice of harvest seasons and best times to collect from your desired plant. Some plants and specific parts of plants may be *toxic* at different times of the year.

- Try to avoid any unnecessary damage to the plants you are harvesting from and the surrounding plants. Watch your step as you walk through the garden. Be sure not to step on any important plants

- For safety, always be 100% positive of the plant's identity being harvested. If you are not 100% sure, consult with an Elder or someone from the Land & Environment Department. Many plants have "look-alikes" that can be toxic.

American bittersweet

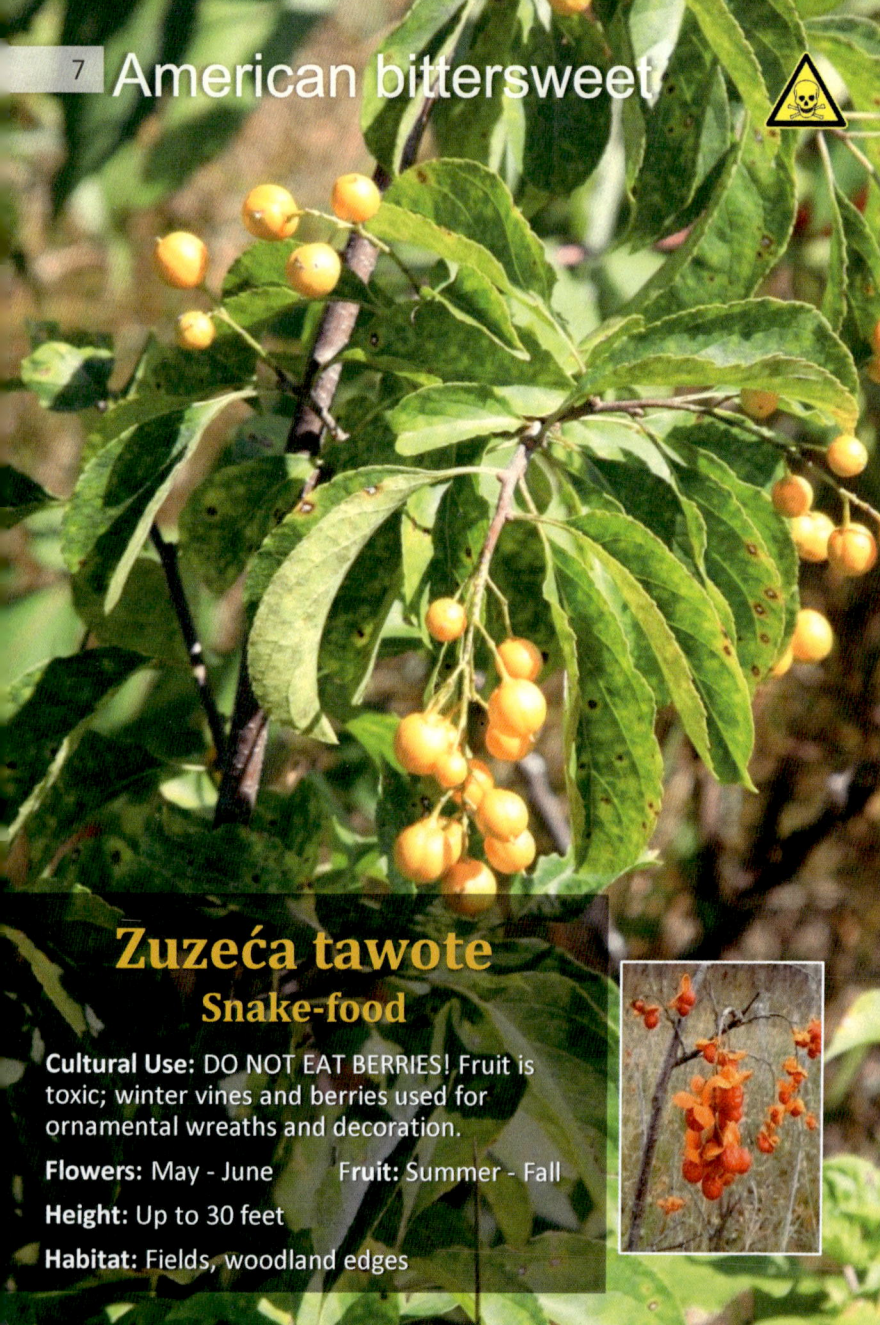

Žuzeća tawote
Snake-food

Cultural Use: DO NOT EAT BERRIES! Fruit is toxic; winter vines and berries used for ornamental wreaths and decoration.

Flowers: May - June   **Fruit:** Summer - Fall

Height: Up to 30 feet

Habitat: Fields, woodland edges

Pe ćaŋ
Elm Wood

Cultural Use: Wood used for fuel, sections of logs used to make huge corn mortars, pestles were also made of this wood. Smaller mortars and pestles used for grinding medicines and perfumes.

Height: 60 - 125 feet

Habitat: Woodlands, floodplains, hedge rows

American hazelnut

Uma hu
Hazel Bush

Cultural Use: Nuts used for food; eaten raw with honey, or used for soup.

Flowers: March – April   **Fruit:** Fall

Height: 4 – 16 feet

Habitat: Fields, open woods, hedgerows

Tewape

Cultural Use: Seeds and tubers used for food. Hard, nut like seeds used with meat for making soup. Tubers were peeled, cut up, and cooked. Tubers were harvested by wading into the water and dug out of the mud with the toes.

Flowers: Mid summer **Fruit:** Fall

Height: 1 – 2 feet above water

Habitat: Backwaters, wetlands

American New Jersey Tea

Taçaŋhutka ṡa

Cultural Use: Leaves can be used to make a drink similar to Asiatic tea. During times of limited timber supply, the gnarled woody roots of this shrub was used for fuel.

Flowers: May - July

Height: 1 - 3 feet

Habitat: Fields, prairies, open woods

Hinta'can

Cultural Use: Inner bark fiber used for making cordage and ropes. Also used for spinning cordage and weaving matting.

Flowers: June   **Fruit:** Summer – Fall

Height: Up to 70 feet

Habitat: Woodlands, riverbanks

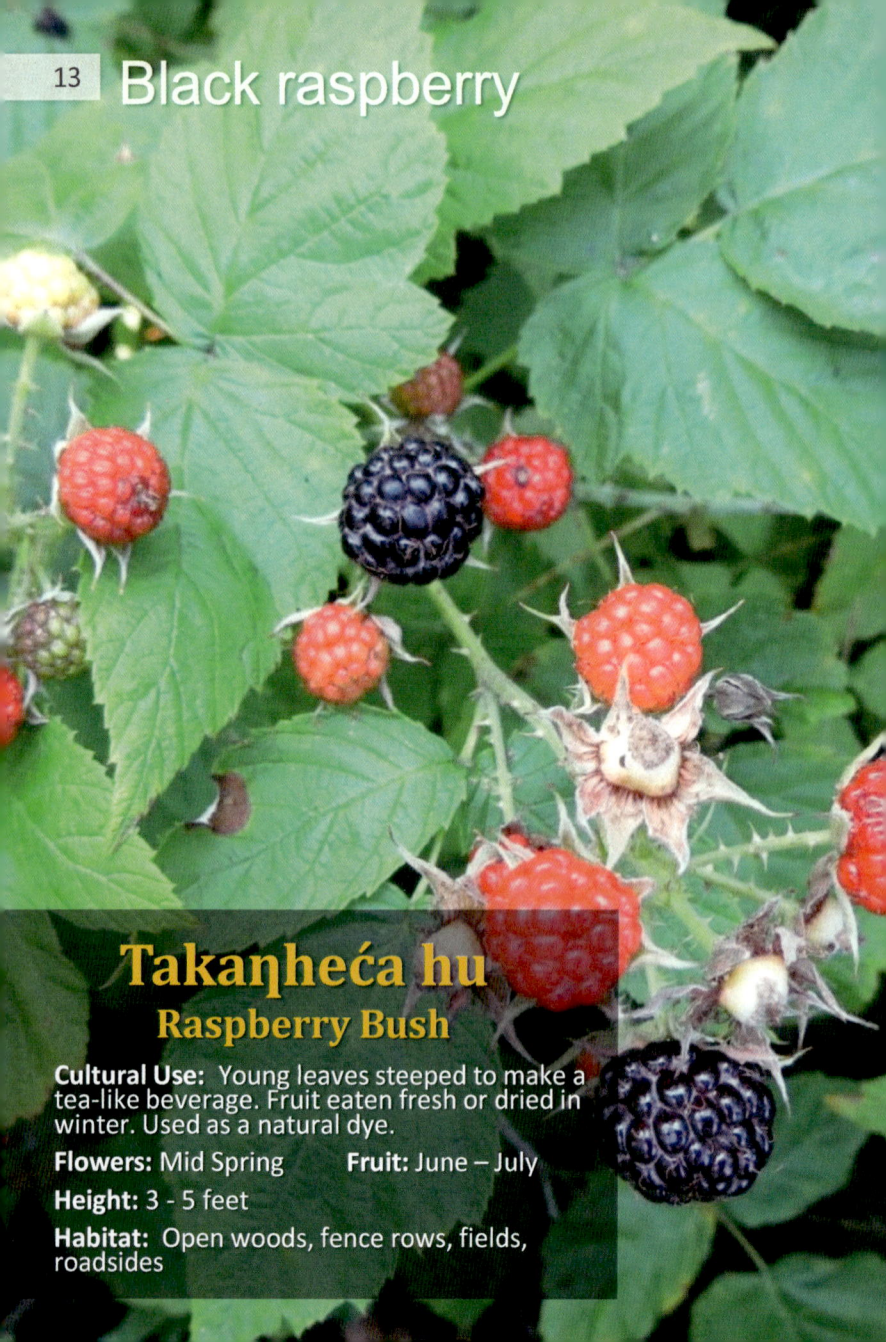

Black raspberry

Takaŋheća hu
Raspberry Bush

Cultural Use: Young leaves steeped to make a tea-like beverage. Fruit eaten fresh or dried in winter. Used as a natural dye.

Flowers: Mid Spring   **Fruit:** June – July

Height: 3 - 5 feet

Habitat: Open woods, fence rows, fields, roadsides

Hma

Cultural Use: Nuts eaten plain or served with honey, or made into soup. Roots used to make a black dye.

Flowers: May – June   **Fruit:** Fall

Height: Up to 80 feet

Habitat: Woodlands, fields, hillsides

Blueberry

Háza

Cultural Use: Eaten raw, dried and stored, or used for jelly, jam, pies, syrup and fruit leather.

Flowers: May – June   **Fruit:** Summer

Height: 6 – 24 inches

Habitat: Open woods, pine barrens, peatlands

Ćahdoġa peźuta

Cultural Use: Leaves boiled in water to make a drink as a remedy for stomach ache.

Flowers: July - September

Height: 2 - 4 feet

Habitat: Wet fields, shorelines, ditches

Box elder

Taškadaŋ

Cultural Use:. The sap, harvested in the spring by gashing the tree, was used to make sugar. The wood was used to obtain charcoal for tattooing.

Flowers: March – April   **Fruit:** Summer

Height: Up to 60 feet

Habitat: Woodlands, floodplains, shorelines

Broad-leaved arrowhead

Pšitoda hu

Cultural Use: Wapato corms (underground bulb, also known as potatoes) are edible. Chestnut sized tubers were used for food, prepared by boiling or roasting until the peeling slips off.

Flowers: June – September   **Fruit:** Summer

Height: 1 - 4 feet

Habitat: Shallow water, wet ditches

Uṭuhu çaŋ

Cultural Use: Acorns leached with basswood ashes to remove bitter taste and used for food. A decoction of root bark is given for bowel trouble, especially in children.

Flowers: Mid Spring   **Fruit:** Summer – Fall

Height: Up to 100 feet

Habitat: Woodlands, prairies

Paŋnúŋpada dúta

Cultural Use: Roots and leaves used in an infusion to treat stomach and kidney troubles, and for sore breasts. A concoction made from the root was used to treat cuts and wounds.

Flowers: June - August   **Fruit:** Fall

Height: 1 – 2 feet

Habitat: Dry prairies

Canada wild rye

Pteyaȟota

Cultural Use: Main food source for buffalo. Seeds edible when boiled with soup or porridge, or ground and used as flour.

Flowers: Early Summer   **Fruit:** July to August

Height: Up to 5 feet

Habitat: Woodland edges, sandy prairies

Čaŋpa

Cultural Use: Fruit eaten by mashing on stone mortars and drying in the sun shaped as small cakes. Important ingredient in wasna, a type of pemmican.

Flowers: April – May   **Fruit:** August – September

Height: 10 – 25 feet

Habitat: Open woodlands, hedge rows, roadsides

Clammy ground-cherry

Ṭamnioḣpi hu

Cultural Use: Fruit made into a sauce, sometimes dried for winter use.

Flowers: June - September   **Fruit:** Fall

Height: 1 - 2 feet

Habitat: Sandy prairies, open woods

Capute
Elder Bush

Cultural Use: Potentially poisonous but cooked fruits are edible. Large stems of bush used by small boys for making popguns. Blossoms dipped into hot water make a pleasant drink.

Flowers: July – August

Fruit: Late summer – Fall

Height: 4 – 13 feet

Habitat: Woodland edges, wet ditches, floodplains, wet fields

Common hops

Çaŋiyuwe waȟpe onapȯȟye

Twining on a tree

Cultural Use: Fruits boiled to make a drink used as a remedy for fever and intestinal pains. A part of the root 3 or 4 feet down was called Makan skithe "sweet medicine" which was chewed and applied to wounds.

Flowers: Mid-summer   **Fruit:** Late-summer

Height: 8 – 40 inches

Habitat: Floodplains, wet fields, shorelines

Paŋnúŋpada

Cultural Use: Eaten at three stages of growth – young sprouts in early spring, like asparagus sprouts; clusters of floral buds; and young fruits while firm and green. Prepared by boiling.

Flowers: June - August   **Fruit:** Fall

Height: 2 – 5 feet

Habitat: Fields, wood edges, shorelines

Common mint

Ćeyaka

Cultural Use: Used in cooking or packing dried meat. Infused into beverages, like tea, for flavor as well as medicinal use to relieve flatulence.

Flowers: Summer

Height: 6 – 24 inches

Habitat: Shorelines, wet fields, hedgerows

Pezuta pa
Bitter Medicine

Cultural Use: Pollen causes allergies. An infusion made from leaves and small tops of this plant can be taken as a remedy for bloody flux; also to stop vomiting.

Height: 1 – 3 feet

Habitat: Fields, roadsides, open woods

Common strawberry

Wažušteca
Strawberry Vine

Cultural Use: Fruit eaten fresh when in season. Young leaves infused to make a beverage-like tea.

Flowers: May   **Fruit:** June

Height: 4 – 8 inches

Habitat: Dry fields, woodland edges, roadsides

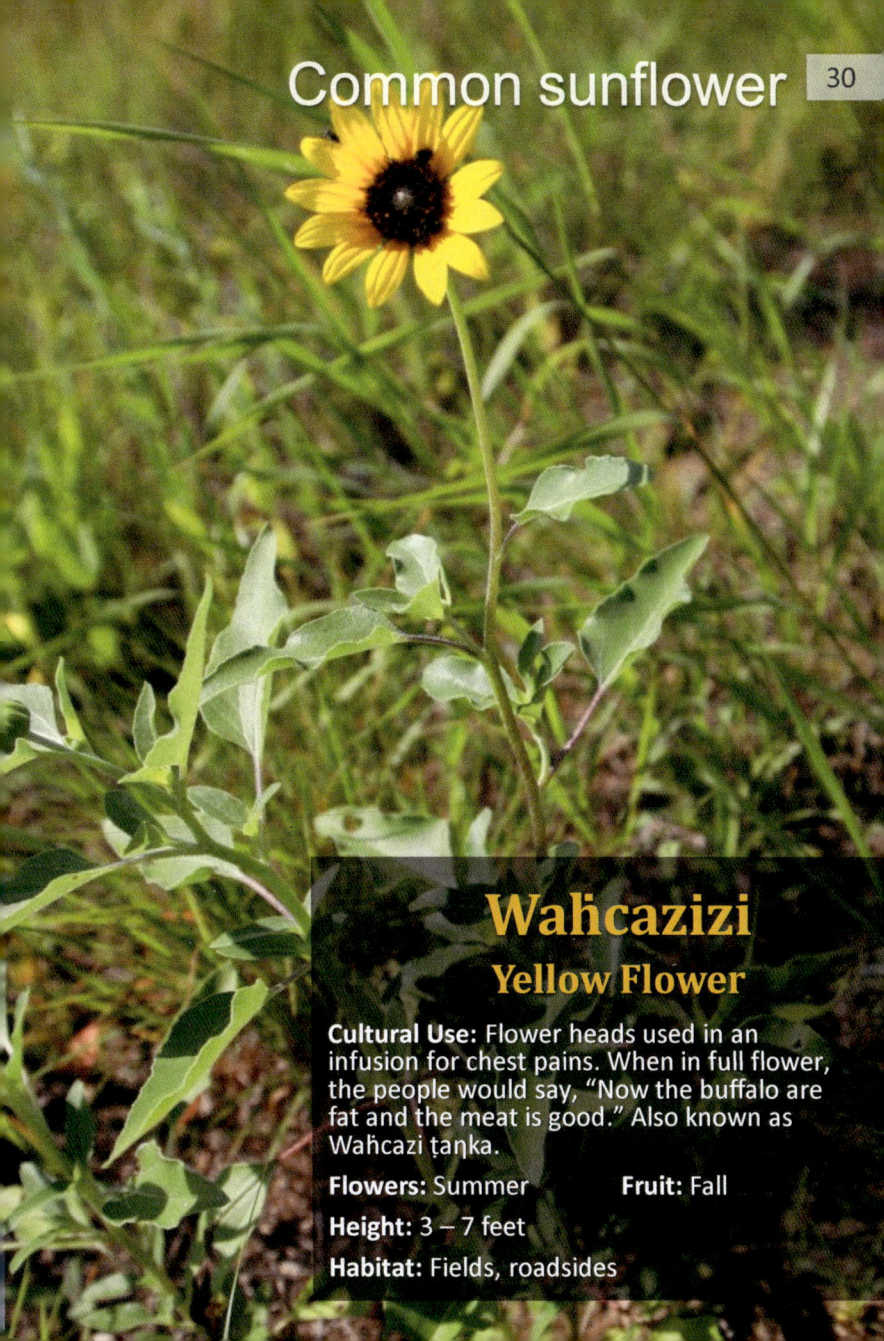

Waȟcazizi
Yellow Flower

Cultural Use: Flower heads used in an infusion for chest pains. When in full flower, the people would say, "Now the buffalo are fat and the meat is good." Also known as Waȟcazi ṭaŋka.

Flowers: Summer   **Fruit:** Fall

Height: 3 – 7 feet

Habitat: Fields, roadsides

Compass plant

Çaŋṡiŋda

Cultural Use: Children gathered chewing gum from the upper parts of the stem where the gum eludes, forming large lumps. Can also be used as a vermifuge (expels parasitic worms) for horses.

Flowers: July – September

Height: 3 – 10 feet

Habitat: Fields, roadsides, railroads

Waǧa ćaŋ

Cultural Use: Inner bark of peeled young sprouts was eaten because of the pleasant, sweet taste and nutritional value. Leaves were used for making small toys and flute-life sounding whistles. Unopened seeds were used as beads by children.

Flowers: March – April   **Fruit:** Spring

Height: Up to 120 feet

Habitat: Woodlands, floodplains

Crabapple

Taspaŋ hu iyeçeça

Cultural Use: Fruit was eaten raw and made into jam, jelly, and ketchup. Also used as trail food and could be dried for later use.

Flowers: May – June   **Fruit:** Fall

Height: Up to 35 feet

Habitat: Edge of woodlands and thickets

źa taŋga

Cultural Use: Root stock commonly used in the smoke treatment for cold in the head, neuralgia, and rheumatism. Also used in the vapor bath.

Flowers: July – September

Height: 3 – 8 feet

Habitat: Fields, shorelines, wetlands

Curly dock

Oskuya

Cultural Use: Crushed green leaves were bound on boils to draw out the suppuration. Leaves were also boiled for food.

Flowers: Mid Summer

Height: 1 – 5 feet

Habitat: Fields, roadsides

Peźuta zi
Yellow Medicine

Cultural Use: Decoction of the root is taken as a tonic; it is used alone and in combination with other medicinal plants.

Flowers: August – October

Height: 8 – 18 inches

Habitat: Fields, open woods

Hokṡi çekpa waḣça
Twin-flower

Cultural Use: Leaves were crushed and applied to cause a blister as a counter-irritant for use in rheumatism and similar diseases.

Flowers: March – April

Height: 3 – 18 feet

Habitat: Fields, open woods

Cedar apple rust:
a fungus commonly
found on cedar

Haŋteṡa

Cultural Use: Fruits and leaves boiled together to make a decoction for coughs. Twigs were burned and the smoke inhaled for a head cold. Boughs were put on tipi poles to ward off lightning.

Flowers: Late Spring   **Fruit:** Summer – Fall

Height: Up to 80 feet

Habitat: Fields, hedgerows, open woods

Evening primrose

Çaŋĥdoĥu huĥda

Cultural Use: Roots are boiled or roasted with new shoots used in soups or eaten raw and used for stomachaches. Flowers eaten in salads.

Flowers: July – October   **Fruit:** Fall

Height: 2 – 6 feet

Habitat: Fields, roadsides, wood lines, stream edges

Ziŋtkada čaŋ

Cultural Use: Shrub was gathered and spread on the ground for meat to be placed and kept clean on, near butchering places.

Flowers: April – June

Height: 3 – 12 feet

Habitat: Wet fields, shorelines, wood edges

Fiddlehead fern

Hiŋhaŋtuŋwaŋ kaȟaȟa

Cultural Use: Spring fiddleheads (top of plant) were cooked by steaming, boiling, or sautéing before eating.

Flowers: Non-flowering

Height: 3 – 6 feet

Habitat: Swamps, shaded hillsides

Psehṭiṇ

Cultural Use: Wood used for making pipestems; also used for making bows, and young stems furnished arrow shafts. Mystic powers are ascribed for ash trees.

Flowers: April – May   **Fruit:** Summer

Height: Up to 110 feet

Habitat: Woodlands, floodplains, hedge rows

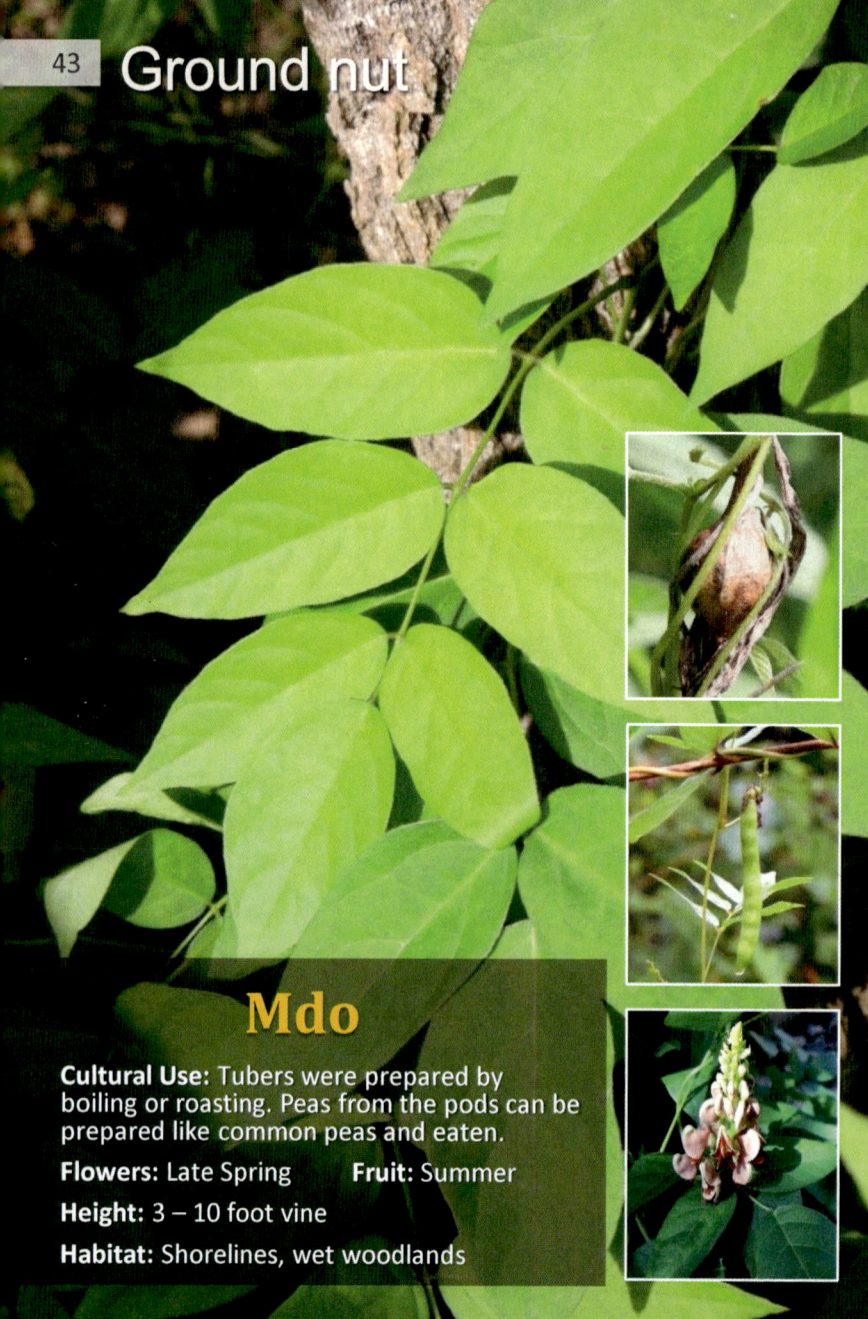

Ground nut

Mdo

Cultural Use: Tubers were prepared by boiling or roasting. Peas from the pods can be prepared like common peas and eaten.

Flowers: Late Spring   **Fruit:** Summer

Height: 3 – 10 foot vine

Habitat: Shorelines, wet woodlands

Pte ṭawote
Food of Buffalo

Cultural Use: Plums sometimes eaten raw and fresh. Caution: similar-looking plants are toxic so consumption without positive identification is not advised.

Flowers: May – June   **Fruit:** Early summer

Height: 4 – 24 inches

Habitat: Dry fields

Ćaŋśiŋśiŋ da
Curly Buffalo

Cultural Use: Tops are used to make an infusion which is given to children for a stomach ache.

Flowers: Mid Summer – Early Fall

Height: 3 – 36 inches

Habitat: Fields, roadsides, railroads

Yumnumnuġapi
To Crunch

Cultural Use: Fruits dried and pounded up for use as a condiment for seasoning meat in cooking.

Flowers: April – May   **Fruit:** Summer

Height: Up to 60 feet

Habitat: Woodlands, floodplains, river banks

Waȟpeto

Cultural Use: Leaves and flowers were eaten raw or cooked. Leaves also used cooked or dried.

Flowers: June – October   **Fruit:** Fall

Height: 6 – 20 inches

Habitat: Bluff-sides, open woods, prairies

Maṭo ṭaspaŋ

Cultural Use: New stems boiled for tea. Fruit eaten raw or used in making jam, jelly, ketchup, and tea.

Flowers: May – June   **Fruit:** Early Fall

Height: Up to 20 feet

Habitat: Pastures, woodland edges, well-drained thickets

Heart-leaved four o'clock

Poípie

Cultural Use: Root was boiled and used as a fever reducer. It was also boiled with purple coneflower root to expel parasites. Root also used as a remedy for wounds, being chewed and blown into them.

Flowers: April – November

Height: 2 – 4 feet

Habitat: Fields, roadsides

Ćahadoga pezuta

Cultural Use: Leaves steeped and infusion is taken for stomach ache.

Flowers: May – September

Height: 1 – 3 feet

Habitat: Fields, roadsides

Makatomnica
Ground Beans

Cultural Use: Large subterranean beans often eaten, as they are tasty and nutritious.

Flowers: Late Summer/Early Fall

Height: 1 – 5 foot vine

Habitat: Wet woodlands

Ispaŋ spaŋheça

Ironwood

Cultural Use: Infusion from bark was taken for diarrhea. Also used as a cough syrup.

Flowers: Mid-late Spring

Height: 30 – 50 feet

Habitat: Understory of hardwood forests

Jerusalem artichoke

Paṇǧi

Cultural Use: Tubers boiled for food, sometimes fried after boiling.

Flowers: Late Summer

Height: 3 – 10 feet

Habitat: Wet fields, hedge rows

Waȟnaȟna

Cultural Use: Seeds toxic to livestock. Bark of root was dried and pulverized, and mixed with water, used as a rectal injection for constipation.

Flowers: May – June   **Fruit:** Fall

Height: Up to 70 feet

Habitat: Woodlands, floodplains, urban areas

Large-flowered beard-tongue

Waȟča ša

Cultural Use: Root boiled and used for chest pains. Plant used as a remedy for chills and fever by preparing a decoction of the leaves and taken internally.

Flowers: May – June

Height: 12 – 40 inches

Habitat: Dry fields, sandy soils

Lavender Hyssop

Waȟpe yaṭapi

Cultural Use: Leaves used in cooking and making tea, as well as a breath mint similar to modern gum.

Flowers: June – October

Height: 2 – 4 feet

Habitat: Dry fields, deciduous woods

Wicahdeśka

Cultural Use: Berries used for food in their season.

Flowers: April – May   **Fruit:** Summer

Height: 3 – 6 feet

Habitat: Woodlands, floodplains, hedge rows

Mna
Black Haw

Cultural Use: Fruits eaten from the hand, not gathered in quantity.

Flowers: May   **Fruit:** Summer – Fall

Height: 12 – 25 feet

Habitat: Woodlands, wet fields, stream sides

Narrow-leaved cattail

Wihuta hu
The Bottom of a Tipi

Cultural Use: Down used for filling pillows, padding cradles, and quilting baby wrappings. Down also used to make dressings for burns and scalds. Tubers used for food and stalks used in weaving.

Height: 3 – 10 feet

Habitat: Wetlands, stream edges, ponds

Narrow-leaved purple coneflower

Icaȟpe hu
Whip Plant

Cultural Use: Used as a general painkiller for coughs, colds, and sore throats. Used as antidote for snake bites and other venomous bites and stings and poisonous conditions. Used as a smoke treatment for headaches. A piece of plant kept over a painful tooth for a toothache remedy. Root was applied to areas of inflammation to relieve burning sensation. Used to increase endurance in the sweat lodge ceremony.

Flowers: Late Spring – Mid Summer

Height: 1 – 2 feet

Habitat: Dry fields

Utuhu caŋ
Oak Tree

Cultural Use: Acorns used for food. Bark of root was scraped off and boiled and decoction given for bowel trouble, especially in children.

Flowers: Mid Spring   **Fruit:** Summer – Fall

Height: Up to 80 feet

Habitat: Woodlands

Waćaŋga

Cultural Use: Used for perfume and burned as incense in any ceremony or ritual to induce the presence of good influences or benevolent powers.

Flowers: Spring

Height: 16 – 36 inches

Habitat: Wet fields, woodland edges, wet ditches

Taŋpa caŋ
Birch Tree

Cultural Use: Bark, shredded fine, was bound in bundles for torches. Also used as material for vessels to catch sap from trees in sugar-making-time, and for various household utensils. Parts of tree used to treat skin sores, burns, to treat dysentery, blood diseases, induce sweating, and to ensure adequate supply of breast milk.

Flowers: Mid Spring   **Fruit:** Summer – Fall

Height: Up to 90 feet

Habitat: Upland woodlands

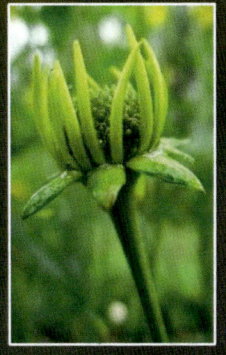

Prairie coneflower

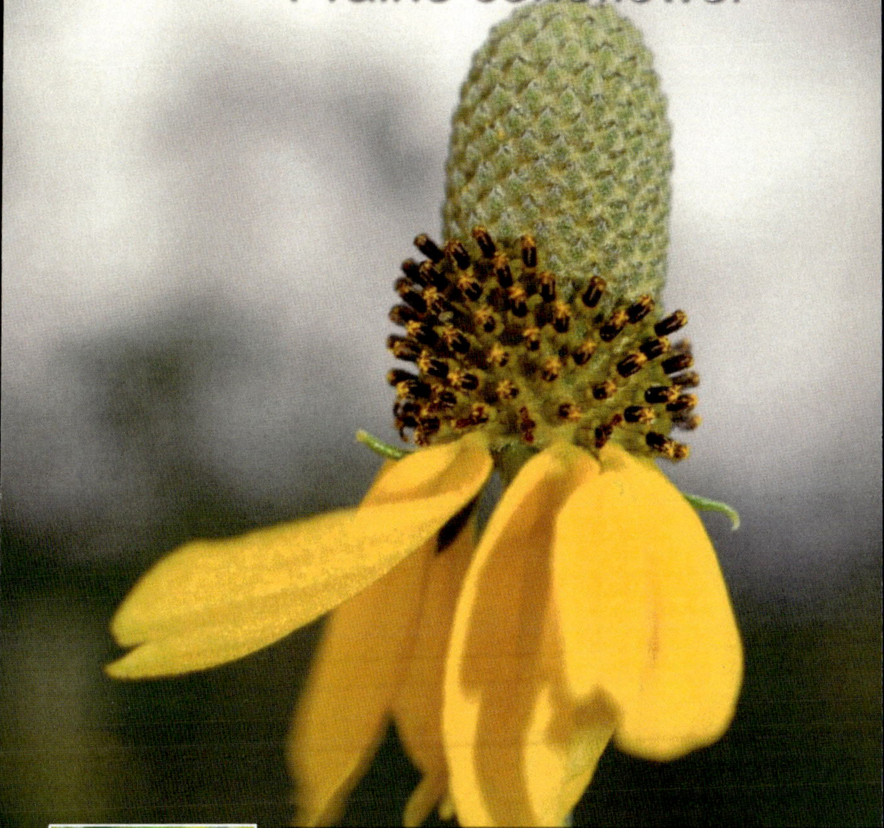

Waȟc̣a zi c̣ikada

Cultural Use: Flowers were used to treat a number of pains such as chest pains and wounds.

Flowers: June – August **Fruit:** Fall

Height: 1 – 3 feet

Habitat: Prairies, dry fields, railroads

Prairie cordgrass

Saŋtuhu Taŋka

Cultural Use: Thatching to support the earth covering of the lodges in the permanent villages.

Flowers: July – August

Height: 3 – 8 feet

Habitat: Wet fields, wetlands, shorelines

Tamaniohpe

Cultural Use: Root used in smoke treatment. A decoction of the root used for stomach troubles, headaches, and wound dressing. Children also used as a toy – inflating the persistent calyx and suddenly striking to pop.

Flowers: July – August

Height: 10 – 24 inches

Habitat: Fields

Uŋžiŋžiŋtka hu
Rosebush

Cultural Use: Fruits sometimes eaten to tide over a period of food scarcity. Inner bark sometimes used for smoking, either alone or mixed with tobacco.

Flowers: Summer   **Fruit:** Fall

Height: 6 – 40 inches

Habitat: Fields, woodland edges, roadsides

Tiŋpsina

Cultural Use: Root peeled and eaten fresh uncooked or cooked; dried for winter food supply.

Flowers: Early Summer

Height: 12 – 16 inches

Habitat: Dry fields, rocky soils

Red elm

Pe'tu'tupa

Cultural Use: Bark, when weathered, used to catch the spark in fire-making. Fresh inner bark was boiled and resulting decoction was drunk as a laxative. Inner bark fiber also used for making ropes and cords.

Flowers: March – April   **Fruit:** Summer

Height: Up to 100 feet

Habitat: Woodlands, floodplains, shorelines

Takaŋhech

Cultural Use: Young leaves steeped to make a like beverage. Fruit eaten fresh or dried for use.

Flowers: July – Frost   **Fruit:** July

Height: 3 – 4 feet

Habitat: Open woods, woodland edges, roadsides

Red Willow

Fall

Çaŋ šaṡa

Cultural Use: Inner bark was used as traditional tobacco when smoking the sacred pipe. Fruits are tart and mixed with chokecherries when eaten.

Flowers: May – June   **Fruit:** Summer/fall

Height: 3 – 8 feet

Habitat: Wetlands, wet fields

Maka ćeyaka

Cultural Use: Infusion of the leaves was used as a remedy for colds. Also used as a flavor and tonic appetizer in diet for the sick.

Flowers: May – July

Height: 3 – 16 inches

Habitat: Fields, roadsides, railroads

Ćaņdi

Cultural Use: Sacred medicinal herb as an (causing vomiting) and poultice (mass of material applied to body to relieve soreness).

Flowers: July – September

Height: Up to 2 feet

Habitat: Open areas

Peżiħota bdaska
Woman's Medicine

Cultural Use: Decoction was used for bathing and taken internally by women when menstruation was irregular.

Flowers: Summer

Height: 4 – 16 inches

Habitat: Dry fields

Sandcherry

Auŋyeyapi ṭaḣpiyoġiŋ

Cultural Use: Cherries eaten fresh or dried for winter, after being pitted.

Flowers: Late Spring   **Fruit:** July – August

Height: 1 – 6 feet

Habitat: Dry fields, dunes

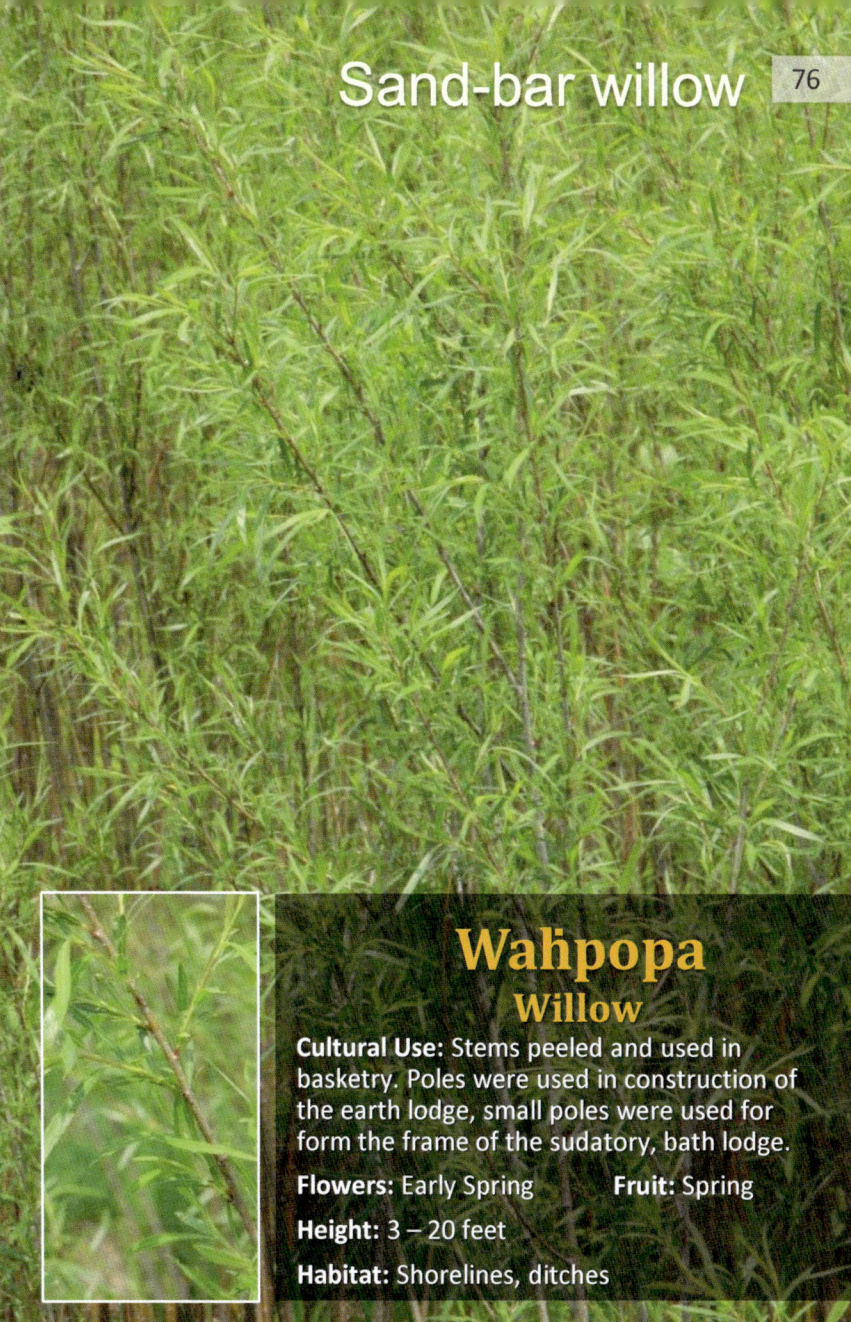

Wahpopa
Willow

Cultural Use: Stems peeled and used in basketry. Poles were used in construction of the earth lodge, small poles were used for form the frame of the sudatory, bath lodge.

Flowers: Early Spring   **Fruit:** Spring

Height: 3 – 20 feet

Habitat: Shorelines, ditches

Wipasuka

Cultural Use: Berries prized for food. Wood used for arrow-shafts.

Flowers: Early Summer   **Fruit:** Summer – Fall

Height: 16 feet

Habitat: Dry fields, woodland edges, sandy areas

Caŋśu
Hickory Tree

Cultural Use: Nuts eaten in the same way as walnuts.

Nuts: Early Fall

Height: Up to 120 feet

Habitat: Upland woodlands, hillsides

Showy milkweed

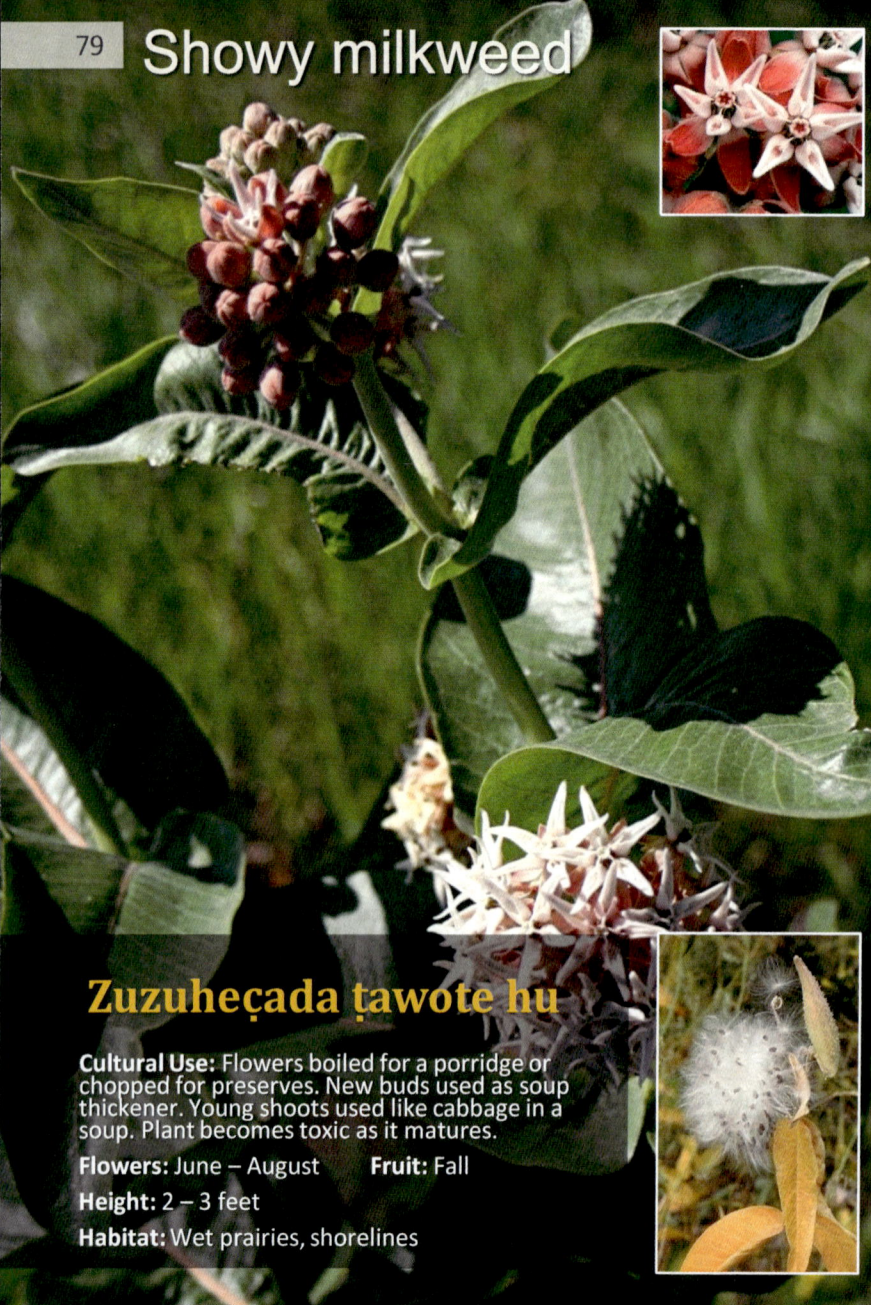

Zuzuheçada ṭawote hu

Cultural Use: Flowers boiled for a porridge or chopped for preserves. New buds used as soup thickener. Young shoots used like cabbage in a soup. Plant becomes toxic as it matures.

Flowers: June – August **Fruit:** Fall

Height: 2 – 3 feet

Habitat: Wet prairies, shorelines

Çaŋ šaša

Cultural Use: The inner bark was dried and used for smoking. An infusion was made from parts of the plant to treat diarrhea.

Flowers: Mid-June   **Fruit:** September

Height: 6 – 10 feet

Habitat: Wetlands, shores

Silver maple

Tahado hu

Cultural Use: Used like Sugar Maple trees for sugar, "sugar water."

Flowers: Early Spring   **Fruit:** Summer

Height: Up to 100 feet

Habitat: Wet woodlands, floodplains, shorelines

Tiçaniça hu

Cultural Use: Root boiled an used a remedy for consumption. In summer, garlands made of the tops of plant and worn like hats in hot weather. Root is said to be poisonous. Also a powerful narcotic.

Flowers: Late Spring – Early Fall

Height: 1 – 3 feet

Habitat: Dry upland fields, railroads

Soft-stem bulrush

Psa

Cultural Use: Tender white part at base of stem eaten fresh and raw. Stems used to weave into matting. Long stems were made into a ball by bending over the base of several together, then braiding the remaining stem for a handle; used in a children's game.

Flowers: Late Spring   **Fruit:** Summer

Height: 6 – 8 feet

Habitat: Wetlands, shallow water, wet ditches

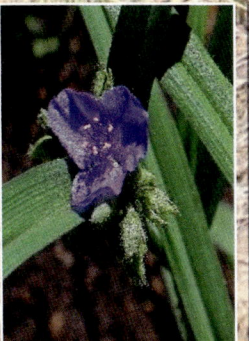

Spiderwort

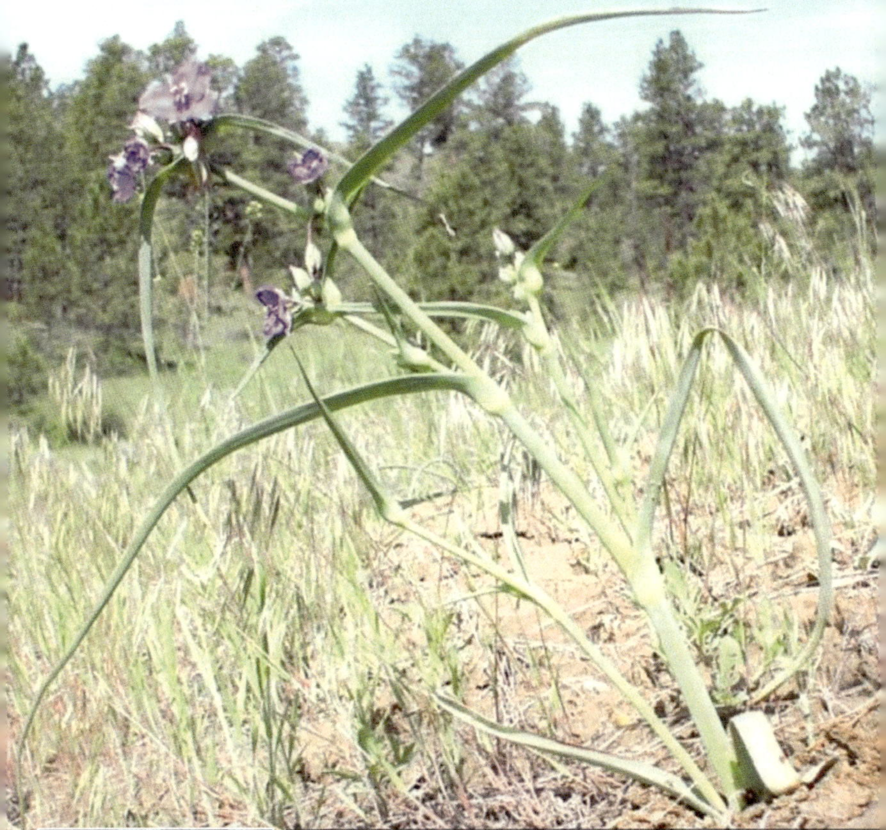

C̣aŋḣdoḣu paŋpaŋna

Cultural Use: Flowers and leaves were collected during the spring and summer and eaten raw, cooked, or dried.

Flowers: May - September **Fruit:** Fall

Height: 10 – 24 inches

Habitat: Prairies, roadsides, wood edges

Çąŋzi
Yellow-wood

Cultural Use: Leaves when turning scarlet in Fall were gathered and dried for smoking. Roots used to make yellow dye. Fruits boiled to make a remedy for dysmenorrhea and bloody flux.

Flowers: June   **Fruit:** Summer – Fall

Height: Up to 35 feet

Habitat: Fields, forest edges, roadsides

Çaŋhasaŋ

Cultural Use: Sugar was made from the soft maple.

Flowers: Mid Spring   **Fruit:** Summer

Height: Up to 100 feet

Habitat: Woodlands

Swamp milkweed

Wahinheya ipiye

Cultural Use: An infusion of the roots was made to make a strengthening bath.

Flowers: June – September   **Fruit:** Fall

Height: 1 – 4 feet

Habitat: Wet fields, swamps, shorelines

White sweet clover

Yellow sweet clover

Waćaŋǧa iyećeća

Cultural Use: Handfuls are gathered to hang in houses for the pleasure of its fragrance.

Flowers: Summer

Height: 2 – 8 feet

Habitat: Fields, woodland edges, roadsides

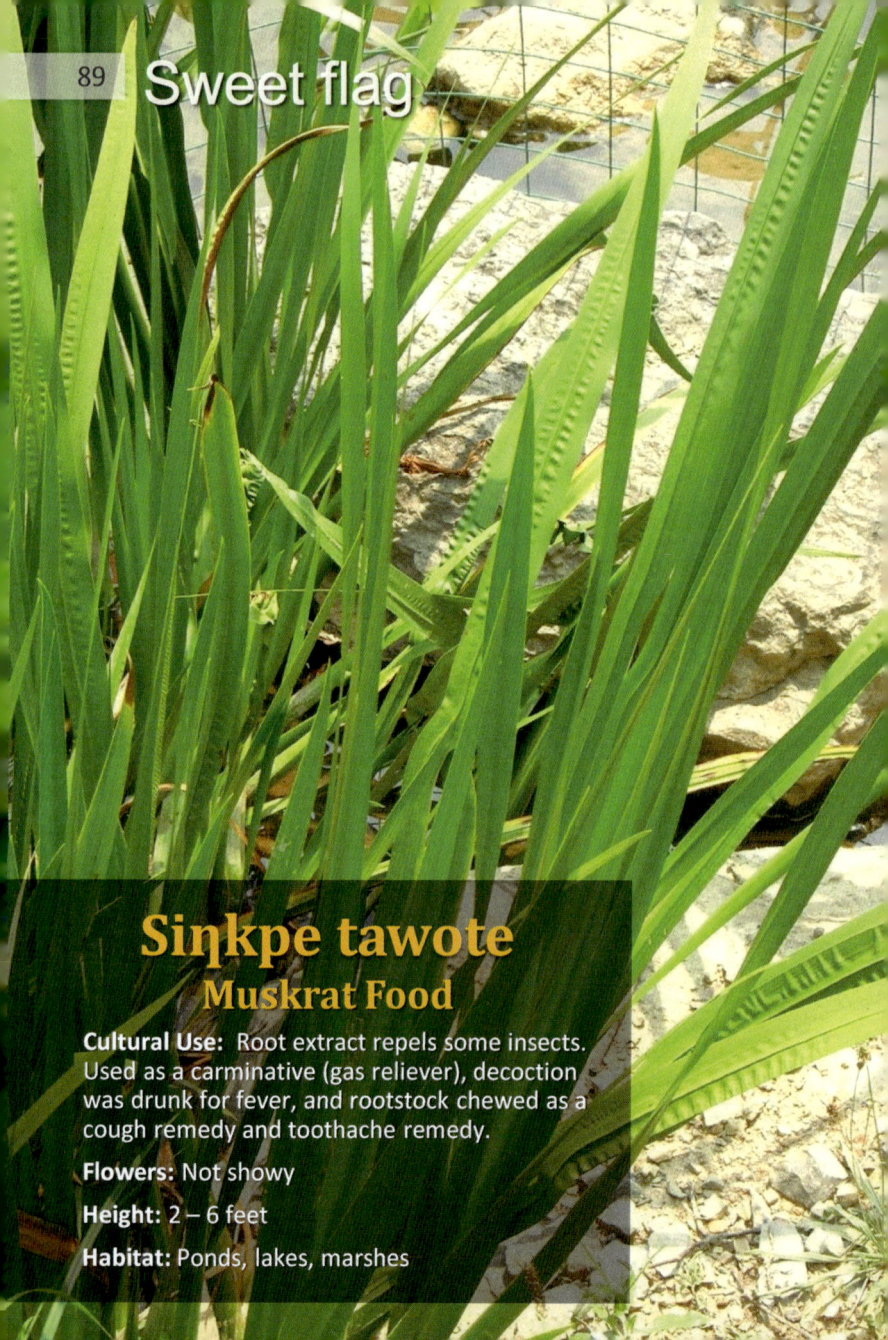

Sinkpe tawote
Muskrat Food

Cultural Use: Root extract repels some insects. Used as a carminative (gas reliever), decoction was drunk for fever, and rootstock chewed as a cough remedy and toothache remedy.

Flowers: Not showy

Height: 2 – 6 feet

Habitat: Ponds, lakes, marshes

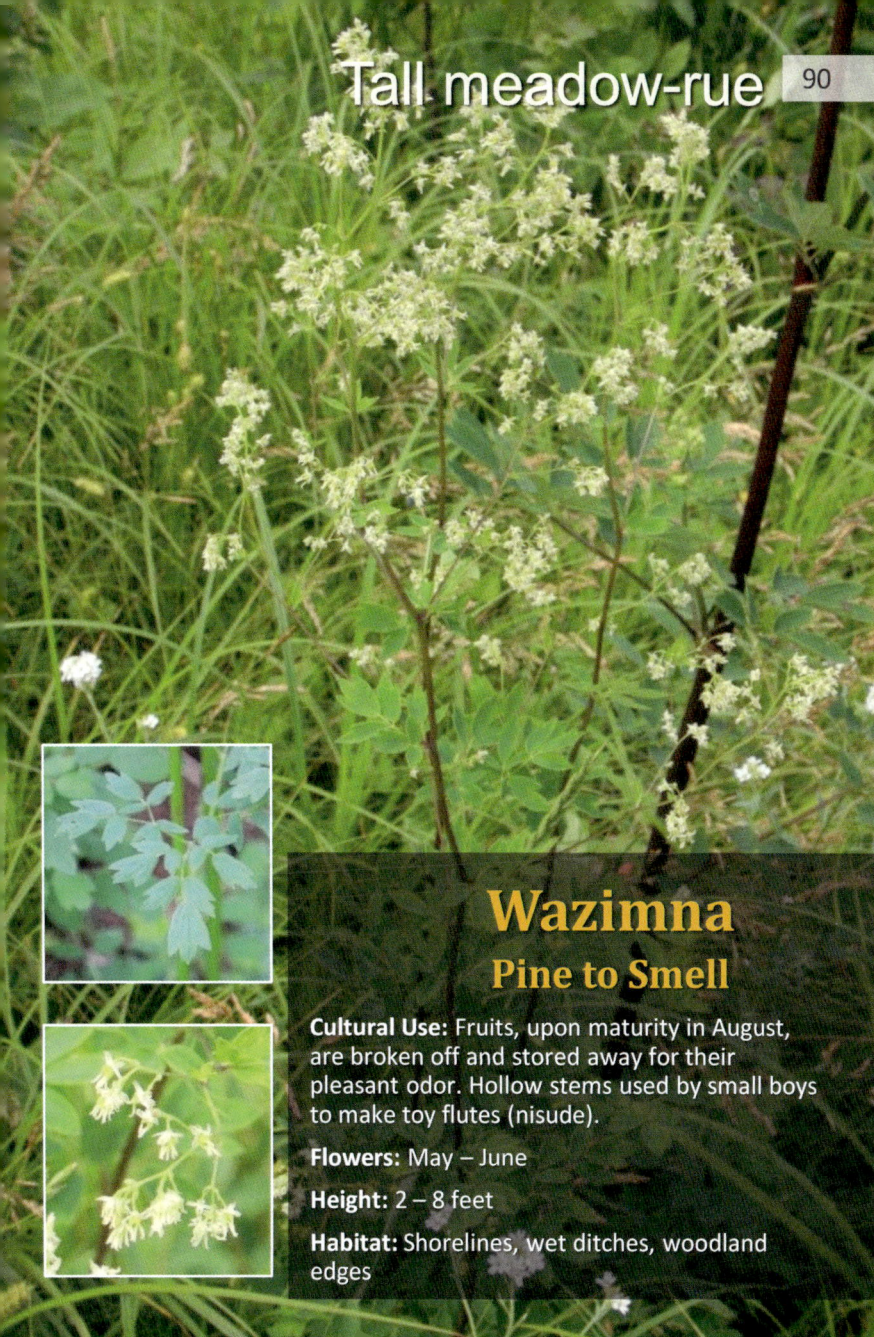

Wazimna
Pine to Smell

Cultural Use: Fruits, upon maturity in August, are broken off and stored away for their pleasant odor. Hollow stems used by small boys to make toy flutes (nisude).

Flowers: May – June

Height: 2 – 8 feet

Habitat: Shorelines, wet ditches, woodland edges

Sakayutapi
Eaten Raw

Cultural Use: Great quantities were planted and eaten raw.

Flowers: July – August

Height: 20 foot vines

Habitat: Dry sandy fields

Zuzeća tawote sapsapa
Black Snake Food

Cultural Use: Eye medicine – infusion of leaves used as was for weak or inflamed eyes.

Flowers: Late Spring   **Fruit:** Summer – Fall

Height: 1 – 5 feet

Habitat: Woodlands

White prairie clover

Ṭoḳada ṭaṗeżuta hu bdoka

Cultural Use: Leaves dried and used in tea.
were dug up late spring/early summer, peeled
and chewed on for the sweet taste.

Flowers: June – July   **Fruit:** Late Summer

Height: 1 – 3 feet

Habitat: Prairie, dry or sandy fields

Waȟpeżiȟota

Cultural Use: A bunch of sagebrush sometimes used for a towel in old times. Decoction of the plant was taken for stomach trouble and many other ailments. Also used for bathing. Often before or during many special ceremonies.

Flowers: Early Spring

Height: 1 – 3 feet

Habitat: Dry fields, roadsides

Wild bergamot

Heȟaka ṭaṗeẑuta
Elk Medicine

Cultural Use: Flowers and leaves boiled together in an infusion to be taken for abdominal pains. Valued as a perfume.

Flowers: July – September

Height: 2 – 4 feet

Habitat: Dry fields, roadsides

Wild cucumber

Wahnahnaheça

Cultural Use: Seeds used for beads

Flowers: July – August　　　　**Fruit:** Fall

Height: 2 – 10 foot vine

Habitat: Wet woodlands, shorelines

Wild Gourd

Wamna peẑuta
Pumpkin Medicine

Cultural Were brightly painted for decorative use. Considered to possess special mystic properties. Had to be authorized to dig or handle it.

Flowers: Summer

Height: 10 foot vines length

Habitat: Field

Wild grape

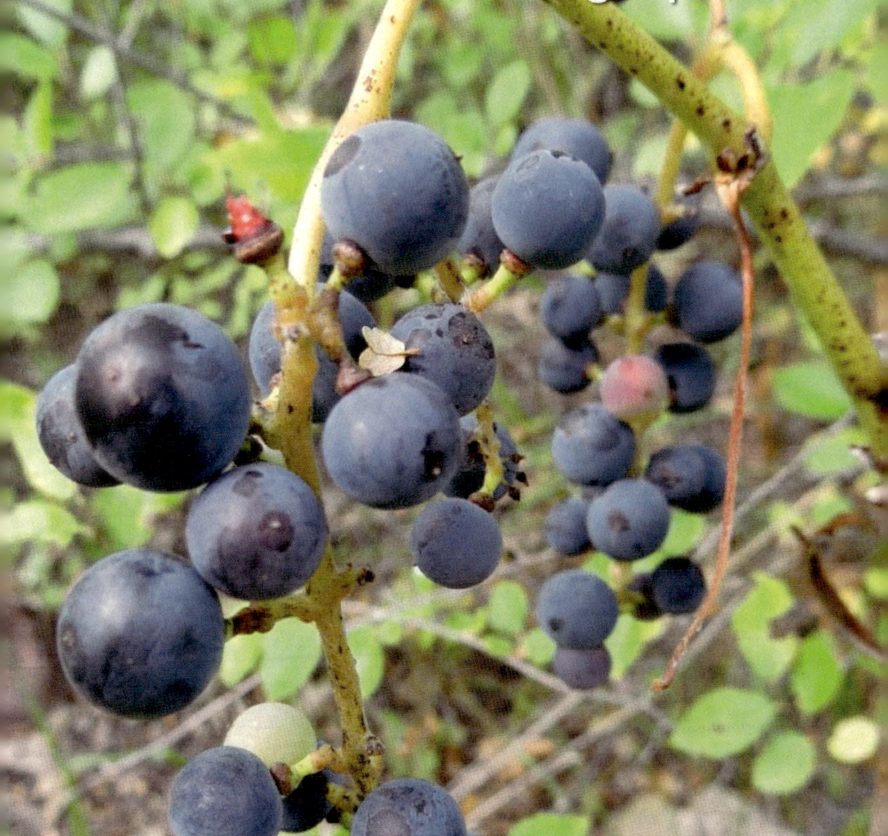

C̣aŋwiyape

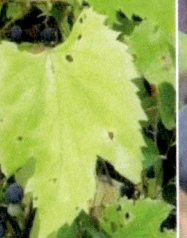

Cultural Use: Fruit used for food, either fresh or dried for winter use.

Flowers: May – June **Fruit:** Summer

Height: Up to 75 foot vine length

Habitat: Riverbanks, floodplain forests, woodland edges

Wild onion

Pśiŋ

Cultural Use: Used for food, commonly raw and fresh as a relish, sometimes cooked as a flavor for meat and soup, also fried.

Flowers: August – September

Height: 8 – 18 feet

Habitat: Dry fields

Ḳáŋta
Plum Tree

Cultural Use: Used fresh, raw or made into a sauce, or boiled and pitted and dried for winter use. Seeds used to make the playing pieces of a certain game in a manner like dice. Brooms made by binding together plum twigs.

Flowers: March   **Fruit:** August – September

Height: 10 – 25 feet

Habitat: Fields, woodlands, roadsides

Wild rice

Psiŋ

Cultural Use: Very palatable and nutritious, to taste, most desirable cereal we have.

Flowers: June – August   **Fruit:** Fall

Height: Up to 9 feet

Habitat: Lakes, wetlands, slow moving water

Wamnu

Cultural Use: Squash used for food.

Flowers: May – June   **Fruit:** Summer

Height: Vines 8 feet in length

Habitat: Fields

Wažušteca
Strawberry Vine

Cultural Use: Fruits used for food.

Flowers: May – August   **Fruit:** Summer

Height: 6 – 12 feet

Habitat: Woods

Made in the USA
Columbia, SC
12 March 2020